In 1933 Hitler became chancellor of Germany and swiftly made himself a dictator by destroying democratic government. He had promised to make the nation great again and to throw off the chains with which Germany had been bound by the Treaty of Versailles at the end of World War I. For the next five years the affairs of Europe revolved around the eruptions, explosions, threats, and promises that issued from Hitler's Berlin. The governments of more stable countries could not make up their minds whether to give in to Hitler's demands (none of which appeared entirely unjust) or to resist them. One of Hitler's grievances, though not a major one, concerned the status of Germans living in Czechoslovakia, a new state created by the Treaty of Versailles. Encouraged by Hitler's proclamation of the greatness of their race, the German minority in Czechoslovakia looked to him for support in their conflict with the Czech government. In the summer of 1938 this conflict reached crisis proportions and Hitler threatened violence against Czechoslovakia. Europe prepared for a general war, but almost at the eleventh hour Hitler agreed to a top-level meeting — in Munich — with the representatives of Great Britain and France, where he drew back from his threatened invasion in exchange for a slice of Czechoslovak territory. The Munich meeting seemed to be a check to Hitler and a victory for peace: it was greeted with hysterical relief in Britain and France. But eleven months later, Europe was at war.

PRINCIPALS

ADOLF HITLER (1889–1945), German chancellor
NEVILLE CHAMBERLAIN (1869–1940), British prime minister
BENITO MUSSOLINI (1883–1945), Italian *Duce* ("leader")
EDOUARD DALADIER (1884–1970), French premier
EDUARD BENEŠ (1884–1948), Czechoslovak president
KONRAD HENLEIN (1898–1945), German nationalist leader in Czechoslovakia
EARL OF HALIFAX (1881–1959), British foreign minister
GEORGES BONNET (1889–   ), French foreign minister
JOSEPH STALIN (1879–1953), Soviet leader

Chamberlain, with his wife, waves from an upper window to the crowd gathered in Downing Street to acclaim the success of his mission to Munich.

MUNICH: 1938

Appeasement Fails to Bring "Peace for Our Time"

By Neil Grant

A World Focus Book

FRANKLIN WATTS, INC.
845 Third Avenue
New York, New York 10022

The author and publisher wish to acknowledge
the helpful suggestions of Dr. Robert S. Short, University of East Anglia, and
Professor Herman Ausubel, Columbia University.

PHOTOGRAPHS COURTESY OF:

Mrs. Hazel Harrison, London: page 28
London Express: page 50
Paul Popper Ltd: pages 33 (top), 54
Radio Times Hulton Picture Library: frontispiece, pages: 2, 6, 15, 16, 22, 27, 30, 33
(bottom), 35, 40, 42, 44, 47, 49, 52, 58, 60, 62, 63, 65, 66, 67, 70, 72
Zeitgeschichtliches Bildarchiv, Heinrich Hoffman, Munich: pages 18, 23, 38

MAPS BY GEORGE BUCTEL

Contents

Munich: 1938

*Neville Chamberlain with his message of peace at Heston Airport on his
return from the Munich meeting of September, 1938.*

Europe Saved?

On September 30, 1938, an airplane landed at Heston Airport, near London, and an elderly man in a stiff, winged collar emerged. He was smiling and holding a piece of paper in his right hand. "I've got it!" he shouted happily to the crowd.

The plane had come from Munich, and its passenger was the British prime minister, Neville Chamberlain. He was returning from a meeting with the dictators of Germany and Italy and the prime minister of France — a meeting that had saved Europe from war over Czechoslovakia. The piece of paper that he brandished was a statement signed by Hitler and himself, which declared that Germany and Great Britain desired "never to go to war with one another again."

Later, happy crowds gathered outside Number 10 Downing Street, and when the prime minister leaned out of a top window, still waving his piece of paper, he was greeted by a burst of cheering. The enthusiasm spread. Policemen laughed when their helmets were knocked over their eyes by boisterous spectators. Two government ministers climbed the railings outside Number 10. Someone started to sing, "For he's a jolly good fellow . . ."

The scene reminded Chamberlain of Disraeli's return from the Congress of Berlin in 1878: "For the second time in our history, a Prime Minister has returned from Germany bringing peace with honour. I believe that it is peace for our time."

Privately, Chamberlain was less confident than he appeared,

and some Englishmen were shocked by the Munich agreement, which they believed had sacrificed Czechoslovakia to the cause of peace. In the words of the poet Louis MacNeice, it was a case of "Save my skin and damn my conscience."

But most Englishmen knew and cared little about Czechoslovakia. Like the prime minister, they wanted peace in their time. They had been rescued, so they thought, from the brink of disaster, and their relief was ecstatic. It was also short-lived. Less than a year later, Great Britain was at war.

The Treaty of Versailles

In January of 1919, the representatives of the Great Powers met in Paris to discuss the terms of a peace settlement. World War I, recently ended, had brought about the slaughter of millions of young men. All of the main participants had been slowly exhausted by the conflict. Only the entry of American troops in 1917 had finally tipped the balance against Germany.

Why had the First World War been fought? Historians have argued at length about this question, but to the peacemakers in Paris the answer was straightforward: the war had been caused by German aggression.

United States President Woodrow Wilson, the voice of morality in international affairs, had no doubts. He believed that the defeat of Germany was a clear demonstration of the victory of good over evil. The representatives of Great Britain and France, although their view of European politics was less high-minded, agreed that Germany was to blame. Their task at the peace conference was to ensure the future safety of Europe, and peace could only be assured by a settlement that would prevent a further outbreak of German expansion.

This could be accomplished in one of two ways: either by a settlement that kept Germany weak, or by a settlement that would satisfy Germany and so remove the causes of German aggression. The Treaty of Versailles was a compromise between these two solutions. Germany was made weaker, but not severely

5

The peacemakers: from the left, Georges Clemenceau, Woodrow Wilson, and David Lloyd George, in Paris, 1919.

and not permanently; the treaty tried to remove some German grievances, but it also created new ones.

President Wilson had promised Germany a just peace. He meant that Germany would be treated no worse than it deserved, but his idea of just treatment was far removed from that of the Germans. They did not see themselves as wrong-doers who deserved punishment. The Germans believed that they had fought

6

only to defend themselves from the hostile powers encircling them. A "just" peace meant equal treatment for Germany. At the least, Europe should return to the situation as it was in 1914, when the war began.

President Wilson found the attitude of the Germans "unbelievable." The British and French prime ministers, David Lloyd George and Georges Clemenceau, found it unrealistic. Public opinion in Britain and France was ferociously anti-German and demanded revenge. It was therefore inevitable that the terms of a treaty worked out by Britain, France, and the United States would be resented in Germany.

The treaty had to settle four basic problems: reparations (the compensation to be paid by Germany to its opponents); the future frontiers of Central Europe; the size of the German armed forces; and the status of Germany's colonies.

The question of the German colonies was relatively simple. Unlike France and Great Britain, Germany had not been an enthusiastic empire builder overseas. German imperialism had been more energetic in Europe than in Asia or Africa. The peacemakers never seriously considered returning Germany's colonies to their former owner, and although they figured on lists of Germany's grievances between 1919 and 1939, the confiscated colonies were never a vital issue.

Setting a figure for German reparations was perhaps the most difficult problem that the peacemakers wrestled with. Astronomical demands were made in Britain and France, but the exhausted German economy could hardly sustain any further exigencies. On this as on other questions, Clemenceau and Lloyd George were compelled to take into account the anti-German feelings of their countrymen, which made the attempt to reach a reasonable

EUROPE 1919–1938

Legend:
- Rome-Berlin Axis 1936
- Rhineland occupied 1936
- Austria annexed 1938

IRELAND

GREAT BRITAIN
London

NORTH SEA

DENMARK

BALTIC SEA

LATVIA

LITHUANIA

EAST PRUSSIA

POLAND

UNION OF SOVIET SOCIALIST REPUBLICS

NETHERLANDS

BELGIUM

Rhine R.

GERMANY
Berlin

Prague

CZECHOSLOVAKIA

Paris LUXEMBOURG

ALSACE-LORRAINE

FRANCE

SWITZER-LAND

Munich

Vienna

AUSTRIA

HUNGARY

ROMANIA

YUGOSLAVIA

BLACK SEA

SPAIN

CORSICA

SARDINIA

ITALY

BULGARIA

ALBANIA

GREECE

SICILY

MEDITERRANEAN SEA

0 100 200 300 400
Miles

N

solution almost impossible. In fact, the peacemakers postponed a final decision. Huge payments were provisionally required, but the final figure was left unstated, and the Germans were assured that no really impossible demands would be forced on them. The payments were to be made over a generation.

Not long afterward, the German economy was gripped by uncontrollable inflation, and by the end of 1922 the German mark had become almost worthless. Germans blamed this disaster on reparations.

The task of redrawing the frontiers of Central Europe was thrust upon the peacemakers of Versailles by the final disintegration of the old Hapsburg Empire, Austria-Hungary. The strength of this ramshackle state had long been sapped by the rising tide of nationalism, and World War I finished it off. In its place, five independent states emerged: Austria, Hungary, Poland, Yugoslavia, and Czechoslovakia (they also included former Russian and German territory).

In theory, these states represented distinct nations, but the population of Central Europe was so mixed up that they all contained groups belonging to different nationalities. Czechoslovakia, for example, contained Germans, Magyars (Hungarians), Poles, and Ruthenians, as well as Czechs and Slovaks. The nation-state principle, strongly espoused by Woodrow Wilson and other liberals, ran counter to geography. It was simply impossible to draw state boundaries on the basis of national groups.

Moreover, in certain cases, the principle was deliberately abandoned. Austria was predominantly German, and many Austrians (including an ex-corporal named Adolf Hitler) would have preferred union with Germany. But such a solution would have made Germany too powerful.

Germans especially resented the loss of population to the Poles and the Czechs, whom they regarded as racially inferior. They were resigned to certain other losses, for instance Alsace-Lorraine, which returned to its former owner, France.

The section of the treaty dealing with German armaments was designed to deny Germany the military capacity to wage an offensive war. The German army was limited to 100,000 men. No tanks, no large ships, and no air force were permitted.

In deference to French fears, the Rhineland was to be permanently demilitarized. This curious arrangement resulted from the absence of any definite geographical barrier between France and Germany. The nearest such barrier was the Rhine, a German river. The treaty forbade any soldiers or military installations in the areas between the French frontier and a line drawn 50 kilometers east of the Rhine.

Many Germans believed that the Treaty of Versailles was unfair and intolerable. Within a short time, other people came to hold the same opinion. The economist J. M. Keynes wrote a book called *The Economic Consequences of the Peace*, which fiercely attacked Clemenceau and Lloyd George and denounced the treaty as absurdly harsh. It made a profound impact on public opinion, especially in England.

Even the hostility of the French toward Germany softened after 1925, as a result of conciliatory moves by Aristide Briand, the French foreign minister, and Gustav Stresemann, his German counterpart. Fears of a revived and vengeful Germany were allayed by France's alliances with the states of the Little Entente (Czechoslovakia, Romania, and Yugoslavia), signed between 1924 and 1927.

Keynes, of course, exaggerated when he painted Lloyd

George and Clemenceau in shades of villainous black. At Versailles, Lloyd George strove for terms that would satisfy Germany, and Clemenceau was a moderate, who was denounced as a traitor by the French rightists because he failed to secure better terms for France. Nevertheless, as time went by, Keynes's statements came to represent the feelings of a great many people toward the Treaty of Versailles. Germans always believed that, sooner or later, the treaty would have to be revised in favor of Germany. Their views were widely accepted abroad.

The purpose of the treaty was to prevent another war. In fact, war broke out just twenty years later. Was the treaty, then, a failure?

By the time the Second World War began, the treaty had long been abandoned by all parties. If its terms had been faithfully fulfilled, Germany would not have been able to embark on a European war in 1939. Whether the treaty was "good" or "bad" is therefore, in a way, irrelevant. The point is that it was not lived up to or enforced.

All international agreements depend on the good faith of the parties involved. The Treaty of Versailles could only be carried out with German cooperation. The Germans were merely told not to build battleships or airplanes. Their government alone was responsible for collecting the money to pay reparations. If the Germans chose to ignore these obligations, there was no way, except force, to make them obey. None of the other Great Powers (except France for a short time) was willing to use military means to enforce the treaty.

In 1919, the League of Nations was set up as the keeper of international peace. It rested on the principle of "collective security," which assumed that the members of the League would

11

combine against an aggressor. Unfortunately, the League proved powerless when confronted by a really determined aggressor like Mussolini or Hitler. The League was also weakened at the start by the refusal of the United States Senate to confirm the Treaty of Versailles. Although President Wilson was largely responsible for the creation of the League, the United States did not become a member. For the next twenty years, the United States vacated the leading role that it had played in Europe's affairs from 1917 to 1919.

Russia, still in the throes of its revolution, had also withdrawn temporarily from the stage. As for the British, they had always disliked continental involvements, and the First World War had strengthened that feeling, while the effectiveness of France had been seriously reduced by internal unrest and slow economic growth. Thus there was a vacuum in international leadership.

World War I had not destroyed Germany as it had Austria-Hungary, and the Treaty of Versailles, despite complaints, did not reduce Germany to impotence. On the contrary, Germany was still potentially the greatest power in Europe. There were more than three Germans for every two Frenchmen, and Germany's natural resources, especially in coal and iron, were far greater than those of France.

Ten years after the signature of the treaty, conditions in Europe were prosperous and, on the whole, peaceful. The new European system had been confirmed by the Locarno Pact (1925), a series of treaties between the chief European countries designed to make the peace more secure. New states like Czechoslovakia, blessed with good leaders, were functioning well. In Germany, inflation had been overcome, and France seemed to be entering a period of relative stability. Old quarrels had been patched up or forgotten. A new generation that hardly remembered 1914 was growing up. War had been ended "forever." The rich were growing richer and the poor were not visibly growing any poorer. People were enjoying life.

It was a brief, sunny interval between thunderstorms. The illusion of peace and prosperity was about to be destroyed by the most disastrous economic crisis ever known.

The Great Depression and the Rise of Hitler

An economic slump normally weakens democratic government and strengthens authoritarianism. This was what happened in Europe during the Great Depression. The German republic was badly shaken; the Labour government was swept out of office in Britain; France tottered on the brink of anarchy. But in Italy, the economic crisis provided an excuse for strict measures, and Mussolini's fascist state flourished in the disaster.

The Great Depression began in America in 1929 and its effects were felt all around the world, most keenly in the industrialized nations of western Europe. Germany, which depended on American loans, was especially vulnerable. Money flowed out of the country and several important banks collapsed. Unemployment rose from less than one million in mid-1929 to more than six million in early 1932. Germans, who had barely recovered from the galloping inflation of ten years before, feared that their country was collapsing into chaos, and government efforts to combat the slump by placing severe restrictions on spending only aggravated the situation.

In the election of 1928, before the slump began, the National Socialist (Nazi) party gained less than a million votes. Four years later, it gained nearly fourteen million, and became the largest party in the *Reichstag* (parliament).

Adolf Hitler, the leader of the National Socialists, was born

Depression: Jobless men gather outside the employment exchange in a British industrial city during the 1930's.

in a small town near the border of Austria and Germany in 1889. He left school at sixteen and two years later went to Vienna, the capital of the old Austrian Empire, where he failed in his efforts to enter art school. For some years he made a meager living painting postcards and spent much of his time in libraries, reading about history and politics. In 1913 Hitler moved to Munich, capital of the German state (*Land*) of Bavaria, and when war broke out the following year, he joined the German army. He served throughout the war with bravery and distinction and

15

The young Adolf Hitler addresses members of the embryo Nazi party in a Munich bar, 1923. This propaganda painting shows the future Führer in a characteristic pose: he used to practice his gestures in front of a mirror.

won the Iron Cross, First Class, an unusual honor for a soldier with the humble rank of corporal.

Although Hitler is often described as a little man, his height and build were about average. He had a penetrating gaze and a rather hoarse voice, perhaps the result of being gassed during World War I.

Soon after the war, he became involved with the affairs of

16

a tiny political party in Munich, and so gained a platform from which he could declaim his political theories.

Hitler's ideas were a mixture of hard common sense and unpleasant fantasy. In his view, humanity was divided into different races, of which the German race was the noblest and greatest. He felt a certain respect for the English, an Anglo-Saxon (that is, "German") people; he despised Poles and Slavs; and he utterly loathed Jews, of whom there was a large number in Germany. Later, Hitler used anti-Semitism as a means of uniting Germans against a common "enemy," but his hatred of Jews was a genuine feeling, not just a political gimmick. Unfortunately, the feeling was shared by many people in Germany and in other countries as well.

Hitler also hated Communists and democrats. His attacks on the German Communists, a large group in the 1920's, earned the guarded approval of conservatives, and his attacks on the German democratic republic were applauded by those who blamed the government for Germany's humiliation at Versailles and its subsequent economic difficulties.

In 1923, Hitler tried to size power in Munich, as the prelude to a march on Berlin. But the Munich *putsch* (revolt) failed, and Hitler spent a few months in a comfortable prison, where he began writing *Mein Kampf* (My struggle).

The failure of the Munich putsch taught Hitler patience. When he came out of prison, he began to seek wider popular support for his movement. Although he was banned from speaking in many German states between 1924 and 1928, his skillful propaganda attracted new recruits.

The Nazi movement had all the militant zeal of a crusade. From the beginning, it included a private army — the SA

A rare photograph of Hitler in the early days of the Nazi party (1925). That cold, dominating stare was to become familiar to millions of people far removed from the "beer gardens" of Munich.

(*Sturmabteilung*), or storm troopers — in brown uniforms, jackboots, and swastika armbands. The purpose of the storm troopers was to preserve order at Nazi meetings. In practice, this meant beating up opponents and harassing Jews.

Why was this allowed? In the years after the Treaty of Versailles, Germany was a violent country. The government was generally feeble; the rule of law was constantly scorned; political assassination was almost commonplace. Bavaria was a particularly lawless state. Ernst Röhm, leader of the storm troopers, used his private army to defend the Bavarian state government and so secured immunity for Nazi acts of violence.

Nevertheless, before 1929 the Nazi party represented only a tiny minority of Germans. The Nazis were energetic, noisy, and sometimes frightening, but they did not appear to be a serious threat to the state. Then came the Great Depression.

The economic slump aggravated the general sense of grievance in Germany. It is not hard to understand the resentment of Germans who remembered the years before 1914. Imperial Germany had been proud, prosperous, and invincible. Then came four desperate years of war, forced upon them, the Germans believed, by the hostility of other nations. They had fought courageously until the armistice, which they regarded as a truce between equals, only to be told that, first, they had lost the war, and second, they were responsible for starting it. The hated Treaty of Versailles was soon followed by runaway inflation, which made their wages, savings, and investments worthless. Finally, a few brief years of growing prosperity and rising hope had ended shatteringly with the economic slump. Economic crisis and political instability once more threatened to ruin the country.

The fog of gloom and discontent was pierced by a hoarse, compelling voice. Hitler promised a new order, a reunited nation, and prosperity for all (except, of course, Communists and Jews). The useless bric-a-brac of the democratic state would be swept away. Unemployment would be abolished. Every German would cooperate in destroying the old sins of self-interest and class prejudice. A new Germany would arise — disciplined, vigorous, and united.

The menace behind this idealistic program was not so

obvious then as it seems now. A great many people were carried away by Hitler's appeal to simple patriotism and duty. Though none of his ideas was entirely new, he was a skillful propagandist and used such modern inventions as the airplane and the radio to spread his message throughout Germany. At Nazi mass rallies, he infused his supporters with a dramatic sense of urgency. At the same time, the activity of the storm troopers increased.

Between 1929 and 1933, various attempts were made by groups or individuals belonging to the German "establishment" to capture the Nazi movement for their own purposes. Conservatives hoped that by cooperating with Hitler they would strengthen their own position and, at the same time, neutralize this dangerous agitator. These "friendly opponents," however, could not match Hitler's energy or skill, and his rapid political reflexes enabled him to turn all their devices to his own advantage.

Thus, in 1929, Hitler formed an alliance with the Nationalist leader, Alfred Hugenberg, in order to oppose the payment of reparations. As a result, the extensive political organization of the Nationalists, which included some very influential newspapers, became a tool of the Nazis. The Nazi party also gained funds from various magnates of business and industry, despite Hitler's attacks on capitalism, because they regarded nazism as a form of insurance against communism.

The electoral success of 1932 gave the Nazis 230 seats in the Reichstag, out of a total of 608. They were still far short of a majority, but it was clear that Hitler could not be kept out of the government. In January, 1933, President Hindenburg, having first consulted the former chancellor, Papen, invited Hitler to become chancellor. Only three of the eleven posts in the Cabinet were to be held by Nazis, and Papen, who was to be vice-chancellor, believed that he would be the real power in the government.

Papen, however, had miscalculated. Hitler had been given his chance, and with his usual ruthless skill, he seized it.

A month after Hitler became chancellor, the Reichstag building was mysteriously burned down. The fire, started by a young Dutch anarchist, gave the Nazis a pretext for attacking the entire Communist party, a potential threat to the nazification of Germany. Immediately after the fire, the Nazi propaganda machine went into action. The German people were told that the fire was the first move in a Communist plot to take over the government. To combat the alleged Communist menace, an emergency decree was passed, giving supreme powers to the chancellor. The governments of the German states were taken over by the central government. Censorship was introduced, political meetings were banned, and hundreds of known Communists were imprisoned. These measures were supposed to be temporary.

The next step was to make the chancellor's emergency powers permanent. To accomplish this legally, Hitler needed a two-thirds majority in the Reichstag. Elections were held in March, 1933, accompanied by blaring Nazi propaganda, parades, and demonstrations. But despite intimidation by the ever-present storm troopers, who now numbered over a million men, more than half the votes went to non-Nazi candidates.

The Nazis never gained a majority in free elections, but Hitler, with a mixture of force and persuasion, did achieve the necessary vote in the Reichstag to confirm his supreme powers.

Old and new: Hitler shakes hands with Hindenburg on becoming chancellor in 1933; the humble bow perhaps concealed a smirk.

The Communist members, and a few other leftists, were imprisoned. Other parties were won over by a show of moderation and patriotism. Overwhelmingly, the Reichstag members abolished representative government in Germany and handed their own powers over to Hitler.

Hitler had won. But potential opponents remained: in particular, conservative and military leaders, and the storm troopers, a huge and unruly force. As the conservatives and the generals chiefly objected to the storm troopers, Hitler was able to win over one side by neutralizing the other, though at some personal cost. The leaders of the storm troopers, including Ernst Röhm, one of Hitler's oldest associates, were executed without trial in June, 1934. A number of other dangerous opponents disappeared at the same time. These acts were carried out by the SS (*Schutz-*

Reviewing the troops: Hitler, with Ernst Röhm, inspects the massed thousands of the Nazis' private army of storm troopers.

staffel), formerly the top division of the storm troopers themselves.

The removal of Röhm and other Nazi leaders reassured the conservatives and the generals, many of whom subsequently supported Hitler. At the same time it removed the danger that the Nazi revolution might outrun Hitler's plans.

The year 1933 was also the last year of the Great Depression in Germany. Thereafter the economy improved. Assisted by Hitler's building programs, unemployment declined and prosperity returned. Political criticism was stilled as the apparatus of a totalitarian state was steadily erected. The SS perfected their techniques and the concentration camps began to fill. The Germans had acquired a strong government.

Hitler, Mussolini, and the League of Nations

Germany had been admitted to the League of Nations in 1926. In 1933, Hitler led his country out again. At the same time, Germany withdrew from the disarmament conference. Hitler insisted that he was in favor of disarmament, but pointed out that the present situation was unfair to Germany. Great Britain, France, and other countries were fully armed, but Germany was not. In order to *dis*arm, it was first necessary to *re*arm! Germany's spending on military equipment at once increased, and eighteen months later, Hitler announced military conscription.

In the turbulent years between 1933 and 1939, the relations among European states were largely decided by Hitler's acts and statements. Hitler's policy was dynamic and determined and it was carried out with skill. In contrast, the policies of Britain and France were static and indecisive and were often carried out with remarkable clumsiness.

It is sometimes said that Hitler had a "master plan" for the conquest of Europe, which was formulated before he came to power and which he put into effect step by step. But Hitler was not a superman, and he could not afford to ignore the rest of the world. He was an adventurer, blessed with speedy reactions. At every turn of the river, Hitler spotted the point to dip his paddle and bring his boat on to the best course. He knew the general direction that the river should take, but he had no map of the currents, the boulders, and the rapids. He had to navigate around each obstacle as he came to it.

Hitler's general ambitions were no secret. *Mein Kampf* was easily available, and the speeches of the *Führer* ("leader") revealed his hopes and intentions. His ambitions were neither novel nor surprising. No German government since 1919 had genuinely accepted all the terms of the Treaty of Versailles. Germany had never reduced its military forces to the level required by the treaty, and under an agreement (supposedly secret) with the Soviet Union, German military equipment had been manufactured in Russia in the 1920's. No German political leader had truly regarded the arrangement in eastern Europe as final: sooner or later the frontiers would have to be changed to take in those Germans who were citizens of the new states. It was clear, too, that Austria, largely inhabited by Germans, should eventually be given the opportunity to merge with Germany if it chose. The demand for *Lebensraum* ("living space") in the east was an old German ambition. Moreover, it was sufficiently vague not to provoke much anxiety, except perhaps in Russia.

Thus, Hitler's general aims in the 1930's were similar to those of previous German governments. The difference was a matter of "when" and "how."

In July, 1934, the Nazi party in Austria tried to seize power. The attempt failed, although the Austrian chancellor, Engelbert Dollfuss, was assassinated. Hitler seemingly had approved the rebellion, but he denied having encouraged it. The union of Germany and Austria was certainly among his goals, but he had claimed he was prepared to wait until it happened naturally. He even sent his regrets to the Austrian government over the death of Dollfuss.

26

Hitler, flanked by the standards of the storm troopers, leaves the Nazi party rally at Bückeburg, 1934.

When the news of Dollfuss's assassination reached Italy, the dictator Mussolini responded by sending troops to the Austrian border. This rather startling event emphasized one of the problems that the Austrian situation presented to Hitler.

The alliance of the two fascist dictators, Hitler and Mussolini, was generally expected in Europe, and it was officially confirmed by Mussolini's declaration of the Rome-Berlin Axis in

1936. Obviously Germany and Italy had much in common, both being, in Mussolini's words, gangsters rather than policemen (Britain and France were the policemen). But they were also rivals, and in some areas, their ambitions clashed. Austria, which bordered both countries, was one such area. Mussolini preferred an independent Austria that acted as a buffer between Italy and Germany. Hitler could not expect Mussolini to look kindly on an Austrian union with Germany. Nevertheless, Mussolini's movement of troops toward Austria in 1934 was probably bluff. It is doubtful that he would have given the order to invade Austria if the Nazi putsch had been successful.

But it was not successful. The first move toward the expansion of German frontiers, though Hitler himself had little to do with it, was thwarted by the prompt action of the Austrian government.

As tension heightened in 1934 and 1935, a flurry of diplomatic activity seized the various governments of Europe. Pacts, treaties, and agreements multiplied. Questions were asked, promises made, and assurances given.

The proliferation of treaties of alliance and defense (none of which was to prove very effective) did demonstrate one fact unmistakably: the principle of "collective security," enshrined in the League of Nations, was inadequate. In various minor ways, the League had done impressive work in the first ten or twelve years of its existence, but the international turmoil of the 1930's revealed its fundamental weakness.

In 1931, Japan invaded Chinese Manchuria, a clear act of aggression. After some delay, the League of Nations declared that Manchuria ought to be returned to China. It did not, however, say how this should be done. Japan ignored the protest,

The League of Nations meeting in Geneva during the 1920's: A noble attempt to introduce morality into international relations, it failed to check those who scorned the principles on which it was founded.

resigned from the League (in the same year as Germany), and later continued its policy of expansion in the Far East.

The League's second, and fatal, failure followed the invasion of Ethiopia by Italy in 1935. Mussolini had no good reason for this extraordinary action, except his desire to show the world, and particularly Hitler, what a great man he was. Nevertheless, Ethiopia was rapidly conquered and annexed. The

League naturally condemned Italy's barefaced aggression, but its words did not worry Mussolini. The condemnation went so far as imposing economic sanctions upon the offender, but they had no serious effect either.

From then on, the League of Nations was insignificant in international affairs. It failed to prevent German and Italian intervention in the Spanish civil war, which broke out in 1936, and when the Second World War began in 1939, no one thought of appealing to the League.

French Problems
and British Fears

The effect of the economic slump in 1929 did not reach France as rapidly as it reached Germany, but the crisis was no less serious. Between 1933 and 1938, while other countries were recovering, France still struggled with economic depression. As wages and incomes fell, popular discontent increased. The governments of the French Third Republic never lasted long in the best of times, and the continuing depression made them tumble even faster. Changing governments meant changing policies: inflation one year, deflation the next. The economy failed to recover and the voices of complaint grew louder. It was a vicious circle. On several occasions during the 1930's, France seemed to be on the brink of civil war.

As in other countries, extreme right-wing opinions gained ground. A number of more or less fascist groups appeared among France's numerous political parties. Some conservatives believed that France needed a Hitler. Instead, it got Léon Blum, a Socialist intellectual, a pacifist, and a Jew.

Blum came to power in 1936 as leader of the Popular Front, an alliance of Communists, Socialists, and Radicals. This unlikely combination of parties, which had never before shown much capacity for agreement, was the result of their common fear of fascism. Blum was in office for only a year, and the Popular Front did not end political violence, which, heightened

Above, a scene during political riots in Paris, 1934: Gendarmes pile up paving stones, the traditional missiles of angry Parisian crowds. Right, Léon Blum, the French Socialist leader who headed the Popular Front government of 1936.

by divided loyalties toward the Spanish civil war, remained a threat to the existence of parliamentary government. However, by 1938 the situation in France was showing signs of improvement. The economy was moving upward, the threat of fascist revolution had receded, and the Spanish civil war had ceased to be a burning issue.

France's internal problems naturally affected its foreign relations. It was difficult for a government that seemed often on the verge of breakdown to pursue a vigorous or consistent foreign policy. Although ministers did not always change when governments fell (Daladier was a member of every government between 1936 and 1940), France's allies were not reassured by its frequent changes of government. In particular, the new states of eastern Europe, who depended on France to hold Germany in check, felt that their own security was threatened. As one Polish leader said, "What is happening in France cannot inspire us . . . above all, this constant fluctuation and lack of determination."

It was doubtful if the guarantee that France had given to Poland and to other states of Europe could, alone, preserve Europe against an aggressive, expanding Germany. It was vital for France, as most of its leaders recognized, to preserve the friendship of Great Britain.

The economic depression was no less severe in Britain than in France, yet Britain escaped the political instability that undermined the French government in the 1930's. The British Communist party was small and ineffective, and therefore did not provoke a particularly fierce reaction from the Right. The British Union of Fascists, in their black shirts and jackboots, succeeded in creating minor riots in London but never became a major national force. The leading political figure in Great Britain

The British fascist leader, Sir Oswald Mosley, admonishes a crowd in Trafalgar Square, London, while his black-shirted bodyguards watch for troublesome opponents.

between 1923 and 1937 was the head of the Conservative party, Stanley Baldwin, a solid, pipe-smoking man who seemed to be happier in his rose garden than in Westminster.

Public opinion in Great Britain during the 1920's and early 1930's was generally favorable toward Germany. Most Englishmen agreed that the Treaty of Versailles was unjust. They sympathized with German grievances and believed that some kind of German expansion in eastern Europe was both natural and

35

inevitable. Even the harsh and violent complaints of Hitler could be put down to justifiable resentment.

Throughout the period between 1919 and 1933, a powerful section of British opinion preferred Germany to France. French attempts to enforce the Treaty of Versailles were regarded as tactless, if not dangerous. The gravest threat to the peace of Europe seemed to be, not German ambition, but French hostility toward Germany.

The political instability of France was seen as another sign of its unreliability. Some British conservatives sympathized with the cry of French extremists, "Better Hitler than Blum," and believed that Hitler, whatever his drawbacks, did at least provide a shield against the menace of international communism.

Hitler Locks
the Garden Gate

Hitler sometimes said that he expected a general European war in 1942 or 1943, but he preferred to achieve his aims, as far as possible, without war. So did the leaders of other European countries, but their aims were to preserve the existing situation, while Hitler's aims involved drastic changes.

It was true that Germany was rearming in the 1930's, an illegal act according to the Treaty of Versailles, but in view of the large French army and air force, no one seriously questioned Germany's right to do so. It was, said Hitler, entirely a defensive precaution. Many people, both inside and outside Germany, were convinced that Hitler desired peace. The violent speeches of other Nazi leaders allowed Hitler to appear as a moderate, even in domestic affairs. He told some British visitors that it was only his restraining hand that was saving the German Jews from much worse treatment.

In March, 1936, German troops reoccupied the Rhineland, an act forbidden not only by the Treaty of Versailles but also by the Locarno Pact, to which Hitler had freely assented. Nevertheless, Hitler's move was not a complete surprise. In the words of a British politician, the Germans had merely reentered "their own back garden," which did not seem unreasonable. Certainly, the British were not prepared to oppose them. When the French foreign minister came to London to inquire whether Great

Britain would take some kind of joint action with France, Baldwin told him that public opinion would not allow it.

French opinion was divided. The premier favored immediate armed resistance, but a majority of his colleagues disagreed. The French generals were also undecided. The French government felt that, in any case, it could not act without British support. So it did nothing.

The effect of the militarization of the Rhineland was to secure Germany's western frontier. As long as the Rhineland was undefended, the French could launch a swift and devastating attack against the heart of Germany. Hitler's action had made that impossible. If, at some future date, Germany became involved in a war in the east (either against the Soviet Union or against the states of eastern Europe), the German "back garden" would be securely locked. France's alliance with the Little Entente became strategically useless.

This was Hitler's most daring stroke so far. His generals had advised against it, and he had to assure them that if the French showed signs of armed resistance he would withdraw immediately. He guessed, correctly, that there would be no resistance. Nevertheless, he admitted later that he had been through the most nerve-racking hours of his life. And Hitler had unusually strong nerves.

Most politicians have since regarded the remilitarization of the Rhineland as a decisive moment in the period leading up to

The Maginot Line, the most formidable system of fortifications ever built, included several underground stories linked by railway; when they invaded France, however, the Germans marched through Belgium.

World War II. Harold Macmillan was one of those who saw the danger. He wrote in *The Star* (March, 1936): "Unless a settlement is made now . . . there will be war in 1940 or 1941. And unless there is a new European system [of peace] built now . . . we shall have a period of frantic rearmament, with intense jealousy and rivalry, which will inevitably lead to war."

In 1936, the German army was not ready for war, and the German generals were no doubt correct in fearing the superiority of the French. But from then on, German military power rapidly increased. At the same time, Britain and France concluded a formal alliance and began to increase their expenditures on the armed services.

Austria Disappears

Hitler accompanied his occupation of the Rhineland with another round of peace offers to Germany's potential opponents. This was a simple propaganda move designed to ward off opposition, and it was becoming clear that Hitler could not be trusted to stick to agreements that did not suit him. Even Neville Chamberlain, soon to succeed Baldwin as British prime minister, remarked that the threat of force was the only argument that Hitler understood.

However, there are only two methods of carrying on international relations: force or negotiation. Since force had been ruled out, only negotiation was left. Despite their doubts, foreign statesmen had to act on the assumption that a permanent agreement with Hitler was possible.

After the Rhineland episode, two years passed without any dramatic developments in Central Europe. Hitler expected the next crisis to occur over Czechoslovakia. Instead, Austria suddenly demanded his attention.

Nazi activity in Austria had been increasing since the failure of the putsch of 1934. An agreement with Germany in 1936 had allowed the big Nazi newspapers into Austria, and two Nazi sympathizers had become members of the cabinet.

The Austrian chancellor, Kurt von Schuschnigg, had many enemies and few friends. The two muscular dictators, Hitler and Mussolini, loomed on either side. Anti-Czech feeling had pre-

Kurt von Schuschnigg, the Austrian chancellor (left), during a visit to London in 1935. With him are the Austrian foreign minister, Baron von Berger-Waldenegg, and the ambassador to Britain, Baron Frankenstein (right).

vented an alliance with Czechoslovakia, despite the fear of Germany that the two governments shared. The Austrians themselves were sharply divided, and Schuschnigg had few wholehearted supporters.

In January, 1938, Schuschnigg discovered a Nazi plot to overthrow his government. Hitler had promised to uphold Austria's independence, so Schuschnigg decided to confront him with the plot and demand a denunciation of the plotters. Hitler was taken by surprise, but showed his usual skill in turning events to his own advantage. Before Schuschnigg could state his case, Hitler flew into a rage, accusing the Austrian government of breaking its agreements with Germany. While the Führer roared, menacing Nazi generals marched in and out of the room. Hitler insisted on new terms for cooperation. A pro-Nazi, Artur von Seyss-Inquart, was to become Austrian minister of the interior with control of the police. Austria's foreign policy should be coordinated with Germany's.

Hitler did agree, however, to condemn the unconstitutional methods of the Austrian Nazis. He was not contemplating the use of force, as he was confident that time would bring Austria into line. Schuschnigg also realized that time was on Hitler's side, and he made a bold attempt to forestall the Nazis by announcing a plebiscite, or referendum, on the question of Austrian independence. This was clearly an anti-German move, for a favorable vote would have ruined the Nazis' case. Hitler reacted, in the words of A.J.P. Taylor, "as though someone had trodden on a painful corn." He demanded the resignation of Schuschnigg and his replacement by Seyss-Inquart, and he ordered troops toward the Austrian frontier.

Although Schuschnigg had given only three days' notice of the plebiscite, the interval was too long. Hitler's prompt reaction trapped him. The British refused to give any advice. Mussolini was keeping quiet. The French were yet again in the process of changing governments. Schuschnigg's own colleagues were against him. He resigned on March 11, 1938.

The next day, German troops entered Austria. They were summoned by Seyss-Inquart (acting on Hitler's instructions) to help keep the peace. Later, Seyss-Inquart telephoned to say the

43

German armored cars on parade in Vienna, following the Anschluss *of March, 1938.*

German troops would no longer be needed, but he was told that the invasion could not be stopped. Hitler himself, who had recently become commander in chief of the German army, joined the troops.

He intended to install a pro-Nazi puppet government that would take its orders from Berlin, but he received such a welcome from the Austrian crowds that he decided to go a step further. On March 13, he had Seyss-Inquart declare the *Anschluss* ("union"). Independent Austria ceased to exist, another clause of the Treaty of Versailles was shattered, and Hitler's ambition to make the German state as large as the German nation took a giant step forward.

Hitler's quick decisions had brought success. He had again gambled that no one would intervene, and again he had won. But even Hitler's strong nerves had been stretched near to breaking point. Mussolini had remained enigmatically silent, and when his message of goodwill arrived on the evening of March 11, Hitler responded with hysterical gratitude that revealed his huge relief: "Tell Mussolini I will never forget him for this . . . never, never, never, whatever happens. . . . If he should ever need any help or be in any danger . . . I shall stick to him, whatever may happen, even if the whole world were against him."

Czechs and Germans

The old Czech state of Bohemia lost its independence at the Battle of the White Mountain in 1620, almost three hundred years before the Treaty of Versailles. Thereafter, it was part of the Hapsburgs' Austrian Empire. The old Czech leaders of Bohemia were replaced by Germans, and the Czech language almost disappeared.

During the nineteenth century, Czech nationalism revived, although hardly anyone then believed that an independent Czech state was possible. Poised between the two largest nations in Europe (the Russians and the Germans), the Czechs supposed that they would have to throw in their lot with one or the other. But World War I weakened the Germans and the Russians at the same time as it destroyed the Hapsburg Empire. Czech leaders seized their chance, and the independent state of Czechoslovakia came into existence.

The new state was a peculiar mixture. The Czechs and Slovaks, although related, did not belong to the same "nation." Their languages were similar but not identical, and while the Czechs were predominantly middle-class, the Slovaks were still a nation of peasants. Although Tomáš Masaryk, the "father" of Czechoslovakia, was a Slovak, the new state was fundamentally a Czech creation. Yet the Czechs numbered only about six million, less than half the total population.

Among other national groups in Czechoslovakia were over

The Nazi Sudeten leader, Konrad Henlein, greeting Hitler; the chubby visage of Hermann Goering can be seen behind Henlein.

three million Germans. Because many of them lived in the Sudetenland, they came to be known as Sudetens. Few of them spoke Czech, although most Czechs could speak German. Government jobs therefore went to Czechs, and the Sudetens felt, with some justification, that they were second-class citizens.

Many Sudeten Germans wanted union with Germany. The Great Depression heightened that desire, for they blamed their hardship on the Czech government. After Hitler's rise to power, pro-Nazis gained ground in Czechoslovakia. Their leader was Konrad Henlein, a physical-education instructor (the Nazis were strangely fond of gymnastics). From 1935 onward, he received financial assistance from Hitler.

Henlein was generally regarded as a moderate. On a visit to England he explained that his aim was to gain more rights for Germans in Czechoslovakia; he did not want union with Germany. The British government urged the Czechs to reach a fair agreement with the Sudetens, but the trouble was that Henlein never said what concessions from the Czech government would satisfy him.

Czechoslovakia's position in Europe was extremely vulnerable. Eduard Beneš, Czech foreign minister and later president, relied on the Western nations to protect Czech independence from German or Russian encroachments. He failed to secure firm alliances with neighboring states, like Poland or Austria, whose position in Europe was similar to that of Czechoslovakia. Beneš liked to think of Czechoslovakia as a bridge between East and West. But when war breaks out on either side of a river, the bridge is the first thing to be destroyed.

Czechoslovakia did have a treaty with France, but after Hitler's reoccupation of the Rhineland in 1936, French aid no longer seemed so useful a deterrent against German attack.

It gradually became clear to Beneš that the anti-Czech propaganda issuing from Berlin was aimed at something more than fair treatment for the Sudetens. He guessed that Henlein was getting advice as well as money from Berlin. An increasing number of Sudetens believed that union with Germany was the only solution for their grievances. At the same time, the Czech government was troubled by nationalist unrest in Slovakia. It was far from certain that the Slovaks would remain loyal in a direct confrontation between the Czech government and Germany.

The Czechoslovak president, Eduard Beneš (left), with an American visitor, the automobile manufacturer Henry Ford.

Hitler's policy was to encourage the demands of the Sudetens and to make difficulties for the Czech government. He did not plan to invade Czechoslovakia. As always, he played a waiting game, confident that a crisis was inevitable and that he would be able to take advantage of it. By the summer of 1938, events were moving in his direction. He put out some diplomatic feelers, sug-

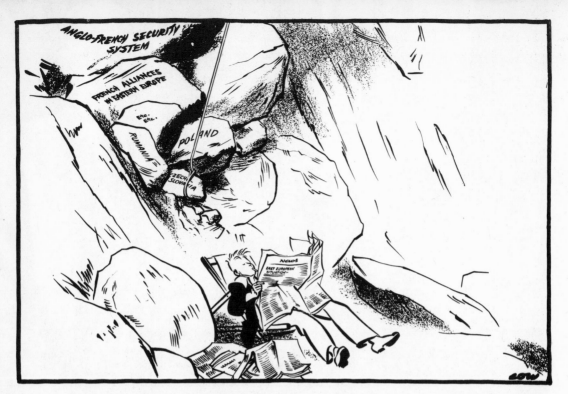

"What's Czechoslovakia to me, anyway?" — *the comment of cartoonist David Low on the British public's attitude toward the affairs of Central Europe, July, 1938.*

gesting to the British ambassador in Berlin that the Sudetenland be transferred to Germany. Perhaps to his surprise, the ambassador, Sir Nevile Henderson, agreed with him. Thus encouraged, Hitler demanded the Sudetenland for Germany in a public speech a few weeks later. The Czechoslovakian crisis was coming to a head.

The Appeasers

Although Czechoslovakia had a good army and strong frontier defenses, it was obviously no match for Germany. Beneš still trusted that the Western democracies, who had created Czechoslovakia, would not stand idle when it was threatened. Hitler, too, needed to know how Britain and France would react if the Czechoslovakian quarrel ended in armed conflict.

In Great Britain, a change of leadership had occurred in 1937, when Neville Chamberlain succeeded Baldwin as prime minister. Both his father and his brother had been well-known statesmen, and Chamberlain himself, since entering politics in 1918, had gained a reputation as a tough and efficient administrator. After the easygoing Baldwin, Chamberlain was expected to bring more urgency and energy to the government.

Although he had no direct experience in foreign affairs (neither had Hitler in 1933), Chamberlain intended to direct his own foreign policy. One result of his determination was that the foreign secretary, Anthony Eden (later Lord Avon), was driven to resign in February, 1938. He was replaced by Lord Halifax, whose views were closer to Chamberlain's.

Chamberlain was not blind to the viciousness of the Nazi regime. Although most Englishmen presumed that reports from Germany were exaggerated, the brutalities of the SS were no secret. Nor was Chamberlain ignorant of Hitler's ambitions in eastern Europe. As early as 1934, he had said that only force

51

The British prime minister, exuding confidence, arrives for a cabinet meeting in August, 1938.

would keep Hitler in his place, but he also acknowledged that Germany's objections to the Versailles settlement were just and reasonable.

Chamberlain's view of European affairs in 1937 was, on the whole, a realistic one. The League of Nations could no longer be considered as a means of ensuring peace in Europe. Neither the United States nor the British dominions could be regarded as likely allies in a European war. The Soviet Union was more problematic. Chamberlain was inclined to write it off. His distrust of Russia was increased by the purges of Soviet leaders that occurred in the 1930's, and he made no attempt to gain a Russian alliance in 1937 and 1938 (and only a rather feeble attempt in 1939).

Chamberlain also had to grapple with the controversial question of rearmament. He believed that Britain was not ready to fight a war in 1938, and that the growing tension in Europe made rearmament essential. But he shared the widespread opinion that an arms race would eventually lead to war anyway, and rearmament, which was also expensive, was not directed very vigorously under his government.

The key to Chamberlain's policy was his horror of war and his determination to avoid it. He had grown up in an era of peace, when few people were old enough to remember what war was like. The declaration of war in 1914 had been cheered by patriotic crowds in European capitals. No one foresaw the ghastly massacre that followed. The impact of World War I on men like Chamberlain was deep and lasting.

In the 1930's, it was widely believed that the next war would be even worse. The new developments in aviation and explosives would make long-range bombing raids possible. Not

Russian enigma: Western suspicion of Joseph Stalin perhaps lost a valuable ally in 1939; Stalin, equally suspicious, made a pact with Hitler instead.

only soldiers would be involved. Civilians would be killed in thousands, probably millions, and major cities would be destroyed.

For Chamberlain, war was the worst disaster imaginable. But he believed that it could be prevented. He was ready to discuss any of Hitler's complaints, and if Germany could achieve its aims in eastern Europe without force, then Britain would not object. Chamberlain believed, no doubt correctly, that Hitler did not want a war with Great Britain.

The policy of "appeasement" (or conciliation) of Germany was not invented by Chamberlain. When the word is applied to the policy of Munich, "appeasement" is a term of reproach, yet the policy of Chamberlain was not basically different from the policy of Baldwin or even Lloyd George. The British government had always been willing to consider revisions of the Treaty of Versailles in order to conciliate Germany.

In seeking a peaceful settlement of European affairs, Chamberlain assumed that there was some point at which all of Hitler's demands would be satisfied. But where was this point? Hitler never said.

Chamberlain was pursuing a chimera. Hitler had no grand design, no final goal. He aimed at the expansion of German power wherever and whenever it was possible. Eventually, it might be necessary to fight. In the meantime, he preferred less-expensive tactics, and the conciliatory attitude of Britain made his work easier.

The Czechoslovakian crisis was not unexpected. The question of the Sudetenland had preceded Austria on Hitler's list of grievances, and only chance had brought the Austrian problem to a head first.

Chamberlain stated the British attitude in March, 1938. British interests, he pointed out, were not vitally concerned in eastern Europe. Nevertheless, if war broke out over Czechoslovakia, Britain would probably become involved. In other words, the Czechs could not rely on British help, but the Germans could not rely on British neutrality.

As a result of the *Anschluss* and the growing tension over Czechoslovakia, talks were held between the British and the French governments. Great Britain and France had been allies in World War I and partners at Versailles, but despite their common interests in Europe, the two countries had drifted apart. After Hitler's occupation of the Rhineland, the British government gave a formal guarantee that if France were attacked then Britain would immediately come to her aid. Military discussions followed, but they ended after a week and were not renewed during the next two years.

The French premier, Edouard Daladier, who arrived in London for talks on Czechoslovakia in April, 1938, had been in office for only two weeks. Nevertheless, this short, thickset man with a jaw nearly as powerful as Mussolini's was an experienced politician. A veteran of World War I, he had played some part (at times the chief part) in politics ever since. In theory, at least, he favored a strong line against Hitler.

Daladier's would-be tough policy was not supported by many of his colleagues, including the foreign minister, Georges Bonnet. Like many other Frenchmen, Bonnet distrusted the British. He also lacked confidence in the military ability of his own country (so did many French generals). He wanted to avoid war at any price.

The talks were not a success. Daladier said that if Hitler were not stopped, he would go on to commit further acts of aggression in eastern Europe. Chamberlain did not disagree, but pointed out that Czechoslovakia was the problem they had to deal with: German grievances were just, and this was not the time to make a stand. Daladier was not willing to match strong words with strong action, and the British view won the day. It was decided to approach the Germans and the Czechs to find out what concessions each side was willing to make toward a solution.

In May, German troops were reported to be gathering near the Czech frontier. Czech soldiers were called up. Two Sudetens were shot, perhaps accidentally. But no invasion took place. The reports of German maneuvers had been false.

Map legend:
- Occupied by Germany October 1938
- Occupied by Poland March 1939
- Occupied by Hungary March 1938 and November 1938

GERMANY

SUDETENLAND

Prague

BOHEMIA

MORAVIA

Occupied by Germany March 1939

Nuremberg

POLAND

SLOVAKIA
German Protectorate March 1938

RUTHENIA

Danube

River

Munich

Vienna

Berchtesgaden

AUSTRIA

HUNGARY

ROMANIA

CZECHOSLOVAKIA 1939

0   50   100   150
Miles

N

    Hitler accused the Czechs of provoking the crisis, and the British and the French were also annoyed. Even Winston Churchill, a persistent opponent of Germany, urged "reason and justice" on the Czech government. At about the same time, a furious Hitler was declaring his "unalterable decision to smash Czechoslovakia by military force."

    The Führer's temper soon cooled. During June and July there was a lull. Hitler was not prepared to risk war with Britain and France over Czechoslovakia.

57

Daladier (left) and Bonnet leave No. 10 Downing Street after a meeting with British leaders in September, 1938.

The British urged the Czech government to give in to Henlein's demand for an independent status for the Sudetens. In August, the British government sent Lord Runciman out as a mediator. Neither the Germans nor the Czechs wanted him, and the French had not been consulted. His mission was a failure.

Hitler was due to address the Nazi party congress at Nuremberg in the second week of September. The British believed that an agreement had to be reached before then. Hitler had, in fact, set a deadline, though a different one: If the Sudeten crisis had not been solved by October 1, the Germany army would invade Czechoslovakia. September was going to be a decisive month.

September, 1938

Although his policy ended in disaster, President Beneš was a skillful statesman. He had outmaneuvered the Sudeten leaders by suddenly offering to grant all their demands. When this failed to satisfy them, it became clear that they did not *want* a settlement. No one could pretend any longer that the quarrel concerned only the Sudetens and the Czech government. Hitler's orders to keep the crisis going were easily deduced.

On September 12, Hitler made his dreaded speech at the Nuremberg party congress. He poured anger and scorn upon the Czechs and demanded self-determination for the Sudetens. The next day, the Sudetens rose in revolt, but the Czech government rapidly suppressed the uprising, and Hitler was denied a chance to intervene.

The British and French governments were in a state of panic. Daladier and others mouthed strong words, but no one was willing to risk a general war. Chamberlain decided to make a personal intervention. On September 15, he flew to meet Hitler at Berchtesgaden.

Chamberlain had never flown any distance before, and he was nearly seventy years old. It was a brave act, but as he said, he was "tough and wiry." He met Hitler alone, except for a German interpreter, and although the Führer ranted and raved at the start, he soon became quite reasonable (Hitler could be extremely charming when he wanted). Chamberlain thought that his word

59

Hitler prepares to speak: the scene at the Nuremberg rally in September, 1938.

could be trusted. On his side, Hitler was pleasantly surprised to hear that Chamberlain had "nothing to say against the separation of the Sudeten Germans from the rest of Czechoslovakia, provided that the practical difficulties could be overcome."

Chamberlain had not bothered to tell the French in advance that he was going to see Hitler. On September 18, Daladier and Bonnet arrived in London to hear his report of the meeting. Daladier again expressed the view that a surrender to Hitler would encourage new demands, but his words were beginning to sound hollow. And as Lord Halifax said, "it would be impossible to give any effective protection to the Czechoslovak state," which would be overrun by the Germans long before British and French troops could act. There were other reasons against resistance: neither Britain nor France was equipped for an offensive campaign (rearmament was concentrated on defense), and whatever happened, the Sudeten Germans would never again be peaceful citizens of Czechoslovakia.

Yet all these reasons were, in a way, irrelevant. The British government was not really concerned with the Czechoslovakian problem, which Chamberlain described as "a quarrel in a faraway country between people of whom we know nothing." Britain's only concern was to prevent a general war.

So France and Britain agreed to the terms arranged at Berchtesgaden, which involved the transference of parts of Czechoslovak territory to Germany. The Czech government, after initial resistance, was persuaded to concur. President Beneš guessed that Hitler would merely increase his demands. He was correct.

On September 22, Chamberlain visited Hitler again. He was dismayed by his reception. The Führer, in a rage, screamed that the Sudetens were being slaughtered by Czech troops. He demanded instant German occupation of certain areas of Czechoslovakia, and he insisted that the claims of Hungary and Poland, which had begun to clamor for regions where Magyars and Poles were a majority, should also be satisfied. These demands, as Hitler anticipated, were rejected by the Czechs.

War loomed. In London, trenches were dug in the parks and gas masks were issued to civilians. Preparations were made for mobilization, while Daladier hastened across the English Channel for more discussions. On September 26, Hitler received a reluctant ultimatum from the British government: If Germany

Chamberlain and Hitler after their meeting in Bad Godesberg: the prime minister seems determinedly cheerful, the Führer, merely bored.

should attack Czechoslovakia, and if France should come to the Czechs' assistance, then Great Britain would "certainly stand by France." Hitler exploded with rage, describing Chamberlain in terms that "could not be repeated in a drawing room." The same night he stated publicly his deadline for the invasion of Czechoslovakia — October 1.

During the next two days, international telephone lines buzzed with distressed appeals for peace. Mussolini, who feared being dragged into war by Hitler, was called in to exercise a restraining influence on his ally.

The British prime minister addressed a crowded House of Commons on the afternoon of September 28. His listeners expected that their country would be at war within a matter of hours. Chamberlain's great efforts for peace seemed to have failed. He spoke of the horrors of international conflict. The gloom was intense.

While he was speaking, his parliamentary private secretary, Lord Dunglass (later Sir Alec Douglas-Home), appeared in the

Merely a precaution: London children trying on gas masks during the war scare in autumn of 1938.

House with a message. Chamberlain paused to read it, then looked up, smiling. Hitler had agreed to Mussolini's suggestion of a four-power conference, to be held in Munich.

"Thank God for the prime minister," someone shouted, and the House of Commons erupted. Members stood on the benches, cheering wildly and throwing their papers into the air. One of the few men who did not join in the general enthusiasm was actually threatened with violence by his colleagues.

The following day, Chamberlain, Daladier, Hitler, and Mussolini met in Munich. Czech representatives took no part in the conference, but waited in another room to hear what the Great Powers had decided.

Another notable absentee was the Soviet Union. Throughout the Czechoslovakian crisis, the Russians had asserted that if France fulfilled her treaty obligations to Czechoslovakia, they would do the same. It is possible that Stalin was bluffing. As Poland and Romania would not allow Russian troops to cross their territory, it was hard to see what practical help the Russians could be. However, neither the British nor the French, nor the Czechs themselves, wanted to become involved with the Soviet Union, especially after Stalin's purges of 1936–37, which eliminated many top military leaders. France and Russia had signed a defense pact in 1935, but neither country ever made use of it. None of the Western powers made a serious attempt to discover what Stalin would really do if they stood up to Hitler. The Munich agreement convinced Stalin that the West was feeble and untrustworthy, and it opened the way to the Nazi-Soviet pact of 1939.

The Munich meeting ended the danger of war. It was therefore a victory for the policy of Chamberlain. Mussolini took the lead in suggesting terms, but the terms had been passed to him in advance by the German foreign ministry. Hitler appeared as an earnest seeker of peace, willing to accept compromise for the general good. He abandoned his threatened invasion. Instead, the "German" areas of Czechoslovakia were to be occupied in stages. The claims of Hungary and Poland were, for the time being, put to one side. (At a later meeting, Hitler and Mussolini awarded a large slice of Slovakia to Hungary, Poland having already seized the region of Teschen.)

Munich was also a victory for Hitler. It was better to gain territory by peaceful agreement than by invasion, and although

The German nation hails its leader: cheers for Hitler in Berlin, 1938.

A mixed reception for German troops moving in to occupy the Sudetenland after the agreement reached at Munich.

an independent Czechoslovakia remained, it was a seriously weakened state. Beneš recognized that Germany had won and resigned as president of Czechoslovakia.

The population of the areas gained by Germany at Munich was more than half German. The remainder, nearly a million people, was mainly Czech, including a number of Jews. Some managed to get away, others did not. Among the Sudeten Germans themselves, there were many socialists and other anti-Nazis. Life under the Third Reich was not to be pleasant for them either.

The German areas also included Czechoslovakia's frontier defenses. Many German generals, who had opposed the invasion plan, regarded these defenses as a formidable barrier. Now they belonged to Germany, and the revised Czechoslovakian frontier was unguarded.

Munich had other disastrous consequences. Stalin was not alone in deciding that Britain and France were "paper tigers." Hitler and Mussolini drew the same conclusion. Once Hitler had favored an Anglo-German alliance. Now he was convinced that the British could be discounted; they would never interfere with his ambitions in eastern Europe. Some highly placed Germans, especially Prussian military leaders who had been both frightened

Daladier (left) with flowers at Paris airport on his arrival from Munich; he was astonished to be greeted by cheers rather than boos.

and shocked by Hitler during the Czechoslovakia crisis, had formed a conspiracy to overthrow him. But Munich strengthened Hitler's position in Germany and the conspiracy collapsed.

The morning after the meeting on Czechoslovakia, Chamberlain asked Hitler to sign his statement to ensure that future quarrels in Europe would be decided by negotiation, not force. He returned to England in triumph and was rapturously received. Daladier too was greeted with cheers and flowers when he landed in Paris. He was astonished. "Bloody fools," he muttered.

The Road to War

The public enthusiasm that greeted the Munich agreement was an expression of relief rather than gratitude. In England, resentment against Hitler mounted, especially after the savage attacks on Jews in November. Then, in March, 1939, Hitler marched into Prague and destroyed the remnant of the Czechoslovakian state. The Czech provinces became part of the Third Reich, and in Slovakia a puppet government was set up under German protection.

After this, even Chamberlain could not list the Munich agreement among the positive achievements of his government. Yet he continued to follow a policy of conciliation toward Germany. He could see no alternative. He deplored the treatment of the Czechs, but if it had not been worth a war to save Czechoslovakia, there was certainly no point in a war after Czechoslovakia had disappeared.

Nevertheless, this was the turning point for the policy of appeasement. Hitler had contemptuously broken the Munich agreement and he had annexed territory that was not by any definition "German." At the time of Munich, Chamberlain's belief that the British people would not accept war against Germany was probably correct. The desire for peace was then overpowering. After March, 1939, this was no longer true.

The arrangement of the frontiers of Poland made by the Treaty of Versailles presented Hitler with several grievances.

Friendly smiles, empty words: The British leaders' visit to Rome in January, 1939, failed in its purpose of applying an Italian brake to the German steamroller; from the left, Count Ciano, Italian foreign minister; Lord Halifax, his British counterpart; Chamberlain; and Mussolini.

The most vital concerned the German port of Danzig. In order to give Poland an outlet to the sea, Danzig had been made a "Free City" with its own democratic government but otherwise under Polish control.

In 1939, Danzig and the adjacent areas largely inhabited by Germans played the same role as the Sudetenland in the Czechoslovak crisis. The Polish equivalent to Beneš was the foreign minister, Josef Beck, who was just as skillful as Beneš and less honest. Unlike Beneš, he succeeded in extracting a formal promise of British support at an early stage in the Polish crisis, although that failed to save Poland from an even worse fate than Czechoslovakia.

The Nazi propaganda against Poland sounded ominously familiar: the Poles, Hitler cried, were persecuting their German citizens. Similar accusations had preceded the *Anschluss* and Munich. The same atmosphere of tension was steadily built up. Ironically, Hitler's case against Poland was better than his case against Czechoslovakia, and the argument used before Munich — that Anglo-French military aid would not save Czechoslovakia — applied equally to Poland. But the opinion of men like Beneš, Churchill, and Daladier had been borne out: Hitler would never be satisfied. The time had come to call a halt.

The German army invaded Poland on September 1, 1939. In accordance with its pledge, Great Britain declared war on Germany on September 3. France followed a few hours later.

The German embassy in London had warned Hitler that the British would fight. Hitler ignored the warning. He believed that Chamberlain would back down as he had the previous year. For the first time, Hitler's gamble failed. His conduct of foreign affairs from 1933 to 1938, though dishonest and immoral, was

71

The failure of diplomacy: troops moving through a French town during the later stages of World War II.

also daring, skillful, and outstandingly successful. But on September 1, 1939, he made a serious mistake. Germany was not equipped to fight a long war. Hitler, although he was already becoming unwilling to face unpleasant facts, knew this perfectly well.

For a time, it looked as though a long war would not be necessary. France was rapidly defeated and Britain forced into desperate defense. Hitler almost retrieved his mistake. But not quite: the planned invasion of England had to be cancelled; the British were not defeated.

Hitler made two more mistakes, equally serious. The first was his invasion of the Soviet Union in June, 1941. The second was his declaration of war on the United States six months later. Together, these three mistakes brought defeat to Germany, and as Russian and American troops marched inexorably toward Berlin in 1945, Hitler shot himself.

Chronology

1933	Jan.	Hitler becomes chancellor.
	Oct.	Germany withdraws from the League of Nations.
1934	July	Failure of Nazi *putsch* in Austria.
1935	Oct.	Mussolini invades Ethiopia.
1936	March	Rhineland reoccupied.
	July	Spanish civil war begins.
1937	May	Chamberlain becomes prime minister.
1938	March	Austria annexed.
	May	Invasion fear in Czechoslovakia.
	Aug.	Lord Runciman's mission.
	Sept. 12	Hitler addresses Nuremberg congress.
	Sept. 15	Chamberlain's first visit to Hitler.
	Sept. 18	Daladier and Bonnet in London.
	Sept. 22	Chamberlain's second visit to Hitler.
	Sept. 25	Daladier in London.
	Sept. 26	British warning to Hitler.
	Sept. 29	Munich meeting.
1939	March	Czech provinces occupied.
	Sept.	Poland invaded; war begins.

Suggested Reading

Gilbert, Martin, and Gott, Richard. *The Appeasers*. Boston: Houghton Mifflin, 1963.

Loewenstein, Francis L., ed. *Peace or Appeasement?* Boston: Houghton Mifflin, 1965.

Robbins, Keith. *Munich 1938*. London, 1968.

Taylor, A.J.P. *The Origins of the Second World War*. New York: Atheneum, 1961.

Thorne, Christopher. *The Approach of War 1938-39*. New York: St. Martin, 1967.

Wiskemann, Elizabeth. *Europe of the Dictators 1919-45*. New York: Harper & Row, 1966.

Index

Italian alliance of (1936), 28-29
loss of colonies, 7
of 1920's, 12, 17, 18-19
1932 election in, 14, 20
1933 election in, 21
pact with Russia (1939), 64
rearmament of, 25, 26, 37, 40
and reparations, 7-9, 20
rise of Nazism in, 14-20
in World War II, 71, 73
Great Britain, 12, 14, 25, 29, 48. (*See also* Chamberlain, Neville)
attitudes toward France, 1930's, 36, 55
attitudes toward Germany, 10, 35-36, 51-53, 69
and Czechoslovakian crisis, 55-58, 59-64, 67-68
failure to restrain Hitler, 37-39, 43, 56, 60-61, 67
French alliance of, 40, 55-56, 62
lack of military preparedness, 53, 61
in 1920's and 1930's, 34-36
policy of appeasement, 54-56, 60-61, 67, 69
and rearmament, 40, 53
relief over Munich settlement, 3-4, 69
and renunciation of force statement, 3, 54, 68
and Treaty of Versailles, 5, 7, 10-11, 35-36, 53, 55
ultimatum to Hitler, 61-62
in World War II, 71, 73
Great Depression, 14, 19, 47

Halifax, Edward Frederick, Lord, 51, 60
Hapsburg Empire, 9, 46
Henderson, Sir Nevile, 50
Henlein, Konrad, 47-48, 58

Hindenburg, Paul von, 20
Hitler, Adolf, 12, 71-73
apparent peace stance of, 37, 41, 65
attitude toward Britain, 67
and Austria, 26, 29, 41-45
becomes chancellor, 20-21
Berchtesgaden meeting with Chamberlain, 59-60, 61
British attitudes toward, 36, 51-53, 69
and Czechoslovakian crisis, 50, 51, 55-65
dismantles Czechoslovakia, 69
"emergency" powers of, 21-24
gambles on nonintervention of Western powers, 39, 45, 71
in Munich Conference, 64-65, 67
and Mussolini, 28-29, 45
1938 plot against, 68
origins of, 9, 14-17
physical appearance of, 16
political goals of, 19-20, 26, 37, 55
political skill and success of, 25, 49, 71-73
political theories of, 17
and possibility of war, 37, 54, 57
and Rhineland, 37-39
rise of, 17-21
second meeting with Chamberlain, 61
signs renunciation of force statement, 3, 68
strengthened by Munich outcome, 67-68
and Sudeten Germans, 47-50, 55, 59
territorial demands on Poland, 69-71
violation of Munich Agreement by, 69
violations of Versailles Treaty by, 37, 45

79

Russia, 46. (*See also* Soviet Russia)

SA (storm troopers), 17-18, 19, 20, 21-24
Schuschnigg, Kurt von, 41-43
Seyss-Inquart, Artur von, 43-44
Slovakia, 48, 65
  a German protectorate, 69
Slovaks, 46, 48
Soviet Russia, 12, 26, 53
  and Czechoslovakian crisis, 64
  defense pact with France, 64
  German invasion of, 73
  pact with Hitler, 64
Spanish civil war, 31, 34
SS (Schutzstaffel), 23-24, 51
Stalin, Joseph, 64, 67
Stresemann, Gustav, 10
Sudeten Germans, 47-49, 56, 58, 59, 61, 66
  charges of Czech persecution of, 56, 61
  revolt of, 59
Sudetenland, 55
  ceded to Germany, 65-66
  Hitler's demand for, 50

Teschen, 65
Totalitarianism, Hitler's, 24
Treaty of Versailles. *See* Versailles

Unemployment, depression, 14, 24
United States, 53
  Great Depression, 14
  and League of Nations, 12
  and Treaty of Versailles, 5-7, 12
  in World War II, 73

Versailles, Treaty of, 5-12, 19, 55, 69
  criticisms of, 10-11, 17, 35, 53
  Hitler's violations of, 37, 45
  lack of enforcement of, 11, 26, 37
  provisions of, 7-10

War, threat of, 37, 40, 51, 53-54, 55, 59, 61-63
Wilson, Woodrow, 5, 6, 7, 9, 12
World War I, 5, 9, 12, 19, 46, 53
World War II, 11, 31, 71-73
  chain of events leading to, 39-40, 69-71

Yugoslavia, 9, 10

ABOUT THE AUTHOR

Neil Grant was born, raised, and educated in England. After receiving a master's degree in history from Cambridge University, he emigrated to the United States, where he taught school and worked for a number of years as an editor for the *American Peoples Encyclopedia*. At present, he is back in England, writing full time. Other books by Mr. Grant published by Franklin Watts, Inc., include *Benjamin Disraeli, Charles V, Victoria: Queen and Empress,* and *The Renaissance* (A First Book).